Rookie
Read-About® Science

What Is Mass?

By Don L. Curry

Consultant
Linda Bullock
Science Curriculum Specialist

Children's Press®
A Division of Scholastic Inc.
New York   Toronto   London   Auckland   Sydney
Mexico City   New Delhi   Hong Kong
Danbury, Connecticut

Designer: Herman Adler Design
Photo Researcher: Caroline Anderson
The photo on the cover shows students lifting a heavy rabbit cage.

Library of Congress Cataloging-in-Publication Data

Curry, Don L.
  What is mass? / by Don L. Curry
      p. cm. — (Rookie read-about science)
  Includes index.
  ISBN 0-516-23619-9 (lib. bdg.)   0-516-24666-6 (pbk.)
  1. Mass (Physics)—Juvenile literature. 2. Matter—Properties—Juvenile
literature. I. Title. II. Series.
  QC173.36.C86 2004
  531'.14—dc22
                                             2004001221

CHILDREN'S PRESS, and ROOKIE READ-ABOUT®,
and associated logos are trademarks and or registered trademarks
of Scholastic Library Publishing. SCHOLASTIC and associated logos
are trademarks and or registered trademarks of Scholastic Inc.

1 2 3 4 5 6 7 8 9 10 R 13 12 11 10 09 08 07 06 05 04

Get moving!

Which of these three things
would be the hardest to move?

The chair and desk would be the easiest to move. The cabinet would be the hardest to move.

Cabinet

Why is the chair easy
to move?

The chair has less mass.
You can push it. It's easy.
You do it all the time.

Why is the cabinet the hardest to move?

It has more mass. You have to work hard to move it.

What is mass? Mass is the amount of matter something is made of.

Everything you can see,
feel, touch, or smell is
made of matter. The more
matter something has, the
more mass it has.

The amount of matter
a thing has will tell you
how hard it is to move.

13

This is Bruno. He is a small bunny. He is made of matter. He has mass.

Here is Princess. She is a big rabbit. She is made of matter. She has mass.

Bruno is easy to pick up. Picking up Princess is harder.

Princess has more mass than Bruno.

Something with more matter is harder to move. Something with more matter also has more mass.

Princess has more mass. She is made of more matter.

Bruno has less mass. He is made of less matter.

Don't be fooled. Mass does not tell you the size of something. Mass tells you how much matter something is made of.

Look at these two things. Which is bigger? Is it the ball or the book?

21

The ball is bigger.

Now answer another question. Is the ball or the book harder to move?

The one that is harder to move has more mass. It is made of more matter.

The book is harder to move than the ball.

The ball is bigger. But the book has more mass.

25

Something with more mass is harder to move. That's because it has more matter.

How can you find out what things have more mass?

First, pick them up. Then, get moving!

29

Words You Know

bunny

cabinet

mass

matter

Index

About the Author

Don L. Curry is a writer, editor, and educational consultant who lives and works in New York City. Don taught for 10 years and has now written more than 50 books on various science topics. When he is not writing, he can often be found in Central Park reading, or looking at the science exhibits at the Museum of Natural History.

Photo Credits

All photographs copyright © 2004 Ellen B. Senisi.